# Bikes, Boards, and Blades

## Tony Norman

GARETH**STEVENS**

PUBLISHING

A Member of the WRC Media Family of Companies

Please visit our web site at: www.garethstevens.com
For a free color catalog describing Gareth Stevens Publishing's
list of high-quality books and multimedia programs, call
1-800-542-2595 (USA) or 1-800-387-3178 (Canada).
Gareth Stevens Publishing's fax: (414) 332-3567.

**Library of Congress Cataloging-in-Publication Data**

Norman, Tony.
    Bikes, boards, and blades / Tony Norman.
      p. cm. — (Action sports)
      ISBN 0-8368-6366-6 (lib. bdg.)
    1. Bicycles. 2. Skateboards. 3. Roller skates. I. Title. II. Action sports
(Milwaukee, Wis.)
    GV1041.N69   2006
    796.2—dc22              2005053681

This edition first published in 2006 by
**Gareth Stevens Publishing**
A Member of the WRC Media Family of Companies
330 West Olive Street, Suite 100
Milwaukee, Wisconsin 53212 USA

This U.S. edition copyright © 2006 by Gareth Stevens, Inc. Original
edition copyright © 2006 by ticktock Entertainment Ltd. First published in
2006 by ticktock Media Ltd., Unit 2, Orchard Business Centre, North Farm Road,
Tunbridge Wells, Kent TN2 3XF, U.K.

Gareth Stevens editor: Carol Ryback
Gareth Stevens designer: Scott M. Krall

Photo credits: (t)=top; (b)=bottom
CORBIS: / © royalty-free 7(t), 15(t). Almay: / © A. T. Willett: 10(b).
Buzz Pictures: 23(t). Red Bull®: 11(t), 13(t), 14(b), 16(b), 17(t), 19(t), 21(t), 32.

Every effort has been made to trace the copyright holders, and we apologize
in advance for any unintentional omissions. We will be pleased to insert the
appropriate acknowledgments in any subsequent edition of this publication.

Printed in the United States of America

1 2 3 4 5 6 7 8 9 10 09 08 07 06

# Contents

# Introduction

BMX bikers, in-line skaters, skateboarders, and snowboarders are all part of the world of extreme sports. They enjoy trying new stunts and practicing until they get them right. These athletes learn to jump, flip, spin, and twist through the air. They never stop looking for new ways to enjoy their sport.

## Basic training

Extreme sports can be dangerous. Stunts on bikes, in-line skates, skateboards, or snowboards, are dangerous. Athletes always wear a helmet and other safety gear. They take lessons, learn the basic skills first, and then move on to more advanced techniques.

## On the increase

Interest in BMX biking, in-line skating, skateboarding, and snowboarding is growing fast. Every year, millions of people try these sports for the first time. Many newcomers not only learn how to do familiar stunts but also develop new stunts.

BMX riders test their skills on rough terrain.

# BMX facts - Did You Know?

Mat Hoffman of Edmond, Oklahoma, is one of the best BMX riders ever. His many skills did not happen all at once or easily. Mat has broken more than fifty bones during his career.

# BMX bikes

# In-line skates

# Skateboards

# Snowboards

Skilled skateboarders can soar high into the air.

Snowboarders and skateboarders do many of the same tricks.

# The X Games

The X Games – originally called the Extreme Games – have been held in the United States every year since 1995. Extreme sports athletes from all over the world come to show off their latest moves. They participate in many different events to win gold (first prize), silver (second prize), and bronze (third prize) medals.

## X Games record breakers

**Skateboarding**: Tony Hawk (USA) completed the world's first successful two-and-one-half, midair spin, also known as a 900, in 1999.

**Snowboarding**: Barrett Christy (USA) became the best-ever Winter X Games athlete in 1999.

**BMX**: Dave Mirra (USA) has won eighteen medals in the X Games Bike Stunt event. In 2005, he won the gold riding a gold bike.

**The Winter X Games have been held every year since 1997.**

**In-line Skating**: In 1997, Ayumi Kawasaki (Japan) became the youngest X Games medalist when she won the bronze at age twelve. She went on to win three silvers and a gold. In-line skating was dropped from the X Games in 2005 because it wasn't as popular as the other extreme sports.

## Skateboarding facts – Did you know?

At the 2004 X Games, in Los Angeles, California, skateboarder Danny Way of San Diego set a new world record when he jumped 79 feet (24 meters).

The X Games helped increase the popularity of stunt skateboarding.

## TRUE STORIES

Los Angeles, California, 2003. Sydney, Australia, skateboarder Jake Brown tried twenty times to do the "900" at the X Games but finally gave up.

Left to right: in-line skating, skateboarding, snowboarding, BMX racing.

# BMX Riding

BMX means "bicycle motocross." It began in California in the early 1970s. A group of kids copied their motocross heroes. In motocross, motorbikers race over tracks of mud or sand, jumping hills and twisting around tight turns. The first BMX racers did the same thing on bikes, and the BMX craze spread worldwide.

## Bike styles

There are three kinds of BMX bike:

**Race:** This style bike works best on dirt tracks. The frame is light but tough, and its knobby tires grip the dirt. It has strong rear brakes.

**Freestyle:** This style bike works great for stunts in skateparks, but is also good for just riding to school. Its tires are mostly smooth, and the front wheel can spin 360 degrees.

**Jump:** This style bike, used for jumping ramps or riding country trails, is a cross between a BMX and freestyle bike. The tires have the most tread of any BMX bike. The knobbier the tire tread, the better the grip.

"Stalling" means holding the bike still for a few seconds.

## BMX facts - Did you know?

Corndog sounds like something good to eat, but for BMX riders, it means being covered in dust — usually because of a fall.

Dirt track racers need a sturdy bike with knobby tires.

## TRUE STORIES

London, England, 2005. British BMX rider Ben Wallace worked with a scientist to create the "Einstein flip" — a bike jump that combines a backflip with a "tabletop" — for a publicity stunt.

Lightweight racing bikes are designed for speeding over rough ground.

The sturdy frames of freestyle bikes make them ideal for doing tricks.

Jump bikes combine strength with a light frame, making them great for dirt racing and jumps.

# High Wheel Action

There are two styles of BMX tricks. "Flatland" stunts take place on the ground and often involve balancing the bike. "Vert" stunts involve riding off a steep, almost vertical, ramp.

## Flatland tricks

Many stunts occur on flat ground.

**Endo**: the rider balances the bike on just the front tire.

**Pogo**: the rider stands on the back pegs, lifts up the front wheel, and bounces as if on a pogo stick.

**Bunnyhop**: the rider "hops" along by jerking the bike up so that both tires leave the ground.

## Vert tricks

Vert stunts are tricks done on steep ramps.

**360**: the rider and bike turn a full circle — 360 degrees — in the air.

**Candy bar**: the rider puts one leg between his or her arms and over the handlebars.

**Tabletop**: the rider leaps into the air, then pulls the bike sideways so it lies flat in the air, parallel to the ground.

**Bikers need a great sense of balance to do flatland tricks.**

## Racing facts - Did you know?

**The first skateparks only allowed skateboards. Now, some skateparks also let bikes share the action. The ramps are ideal for BMX vert stunts.**

A rider performing a "cancan" flips one leg over the frame so that both legs are on the same side of the bike.

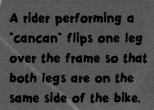

# TRUE STORIES

San Francisco, California, 2000. BMX star Dave Mirra of Greenville, North Carolina, wins the **X Games** gold medal for a double backflip.

**wall ramp**

**fun box**

**pyramid corner**

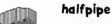

**halfpipe**

# Dirt Jumping

Dirt jumping tracks are made of mounds of mud piled into different shapes and heights. BMX riders ride up one mound, fly through the air, then attempt to land on another mound. They must approach the first mound at a high enough speed to get airborne, then do a stunt in midair before landing on the next mound.

## Dirt-bike jumping stunts

Top dirt-bike jumpers can do forward and back flips on their bikes as they speed through the air. The Superman seatgrab is another dirt-bike trick. The rider comes off the bike in midair and holds his or her body straight out like Superman.

## No limits

In X Games BMX dirt-bike jumping contests, riders make a total of three runs around a course. These are contests of skill instead of speed. The rider who does the hardest tricks and jumps with the most skill wins.

Trail riders encounter many jumps as they follow a course through woods.

## Racing facts - Did you know?

The dips between the mounds on a dirt-bike jumping course are called canyons. Riders might rise 13 feet (4 meters) above the canyons at the top of their jumps.

Benny Korthaus of Germering, Germany, performs the Superman seatgrab trick.

## TRUE STORIES

BMX dirt track racing will be an Olympic sport for the first time in Beijing, China, in 2008.

ABA (American Bicycle Association) rules require that competitors wear:

enclosed shoes (not sandals)

a long-sleeved shirt (or short sleeves with elbow pads)

long pants (even if the rider is also wearing knee and shin pads)

a helmet (a faceguard is recommended but not required)

# In-line Skating History

The first in-line skates were made in the 1700s in Holland (now the Netherlands). The skates had wooden wheels. Today's skates have four or five plastic wheels, all in a straight line.

## Hockey training

Brothers Scott and Brennan Olson from Minneapolis, Minnesota, made the first modern in-line skates. They played ice hockey, but wanted to train in the summer, too. The Olsons removed the blades from their ice skates and added wheels and a brake. Their company, Rollerblade Inc., is now worldwide, and millions of people incorrectly call this sport "rollerblading."

## In-line skating stunts

Stunt skates have four small, hard wheels that make them ideal for performing jumps and stunts. Plastic or metal "grind plates" along the sides protect the wheels when the skates are used for stunts.

This skater balances on the coping, the metal strip at the top of a ramp.

## In-line skater facts - Did you know?

In-line skaters enter many different kinds of races. For example, about six competitors at a time race in sprints that are about 547 yards (500 m) long. Distance races might be 15 miles (25 kilometers) long.

Vert ramps, like this one, are usually
about 10 feet (3 meters) high.

## TRUE STORIES

London, England, 1760. Joseph Merlin built in-
line skates with metal wheels. He wore them
to a party and crashed into a big mirror.
He did not know how to stop!

Recreational
skates are
comfortable
and durable,
ideal for skateparks.

Racing skates have five
wheels and are built for
maximum speed.

Sturdy stunt
skates protect
the feet
during tricks.

# Blade Running

Like BMX riders, in-line skaters are now welcome at most skateparks. They use the ramps to perform many stunts.

## Skatepark ramps

In-line skaters use the halfpipe (a U-shaped ramp that looks like half a pipe), the vert (a ramp so steep it becomes vertical), and the coping (a metal strip at the top of the halfpipe wall) for doing tricks.

## In-line stunts

**Invert**: The skater travels up the wall, then holds onto the coping at the top edge and does a handstand. The legs may be bent or straight.

**Front flip on vert**: The skater travels up the vert backward, then does a front flip in midair before landing and skating back down facing forward.

**Railslide**: The skater slides down a rail using the grind plates alongside the skate wheels.

**Grind**: The skater uses the grind plates to balance a ledge, rail, coping, or other object without touching the wheels. As the skater travels downward, he or she may complete the trick with a double spin.

**A skater grabs the coping to make a turn.**

## In-line skater facts - Did you know?

In-line skaters keep their sense of humor, even if they get hurt. They refer to the scraps and bruises from a fall as "road rash."

Tomasz Piekarski,
of Warsaw, Poland,
performs a railslide.

## TRUE STORIES

Girls who skate look up to Sao Paulo, Brazil, native Fabiola da Silva. Fabiola has won more X Games medals than any other female in-line skater.

| helmet | elbow pads | knee pads | gloves | wrist guards |
|---|---|---|---|---|

# Land Surfing

Skateboarding began in the United States in the 1950s. It did not become popular until the 1970s, when kids in California began skateboarding in empty swimming pools. They compared it to surfing on dry land.

## Best boards

The first skateboards were wide and had clay wheels that were hard to control. Modern boards are usually made of maple, which is a very flexible type of wood. Wheels are made from a hard plastic called polyurethane.

## Top move

Alan Gelfand invented the "ollie" in the early 1980s. Mastering the ollie is key to learning other tricks. The ollie looks easy but is hard to do — while kicking down on the back of the board, the skater must slide the other foot up the middle as he or she jumps into the air. When done correctly, the ollie makes it look as if the board is glued to the skateboarder's feet.

**Keeping control of the board is the mark of a great rider.**

## Skateboard facts - Did you know?

Danny Wainwright of Bristol, England, holds the world record for the highest ollie. In 2000, at the Ollie Challenge in Long Beach, California, he jumped 44.5 inches (113 centimeters).

Udi Hason of Bat Yam, Israel, performs a handrail grind at the Street Dogs competition in Rome, Italy.

## TRUE STORIES

Fountain Hills, Arizona, 1998. Gary Hardwick from Carlsbad, California, sets the record for fastest skateboard run ever: 63 miles (101 kilometers) per hour.

Many skateboarders like to make their own boards.

The deck designs can get crazy.

Each board has two "trucks" that hold the wheels.

Wheels come in many sizes and colors.

Bearings, nuts, and bolts bring it all together.

# Know Fear

For some stunts, skateboarders launch themselves into the air by jumping off stairs or rails or moving fast up a ramp. There is no time for fear. Safety gear, such as a helmet and knee, elbow, and wrist pads, helps prevent injuries.

## Wipeout

Skateboarders do not fall — they "wipeout." They often tease each other about the wipeouts. Experienced skateboarders know that the best way to deal with a wipeout is to simply relax and roll.

## Advanced stunts

**Kick flip**: While doing an ollie, flip the board around in midair before landing.

**Grind**: After an ollie, land with an edge, curb, or other obstacle between the wheels. Slide down while balancing on the trucks. Do another ollie to come off the obstacle.

**Kick turn**: Push gently up a slope. At the top, kick down on the back wheels to lift the front wheels and make a 180-degree-turn to face the opposite direction.

**Rock and roll**: Rock the board on the edge of a curb, ledge, or railing. End with a kick turn.

Skateboarders invent and practice new stunts at Skater's Point in Santa Barbara, California.

## Skateboard facts - Did you know?

Regular or goofy foot? "Regular" skaters put their left foot toward the front of the board. "Goofy" skaters put their right foot forward. Skaters just do what feels best.

# TRUE STORIES

World-famous skateboarder Andy MacDonald now lives in San Diego, California. His advice is simple: "Don't do things to be 'cool.' Do what you want to do. Above all, have fun!"

Sandro Dias of Sao Paulo, Brazil, practices for a competition in Rio de Janeiro, Brazil.

Skateboarders build or buy equipment to help them practice.

Grind rail. This one is 6 feet (1.8 m) long.

A portable ramp with a textured surface provides grip for wheels

Skateboarding tape is called griptape. A rough upper surface helps riders keep their feet on the board.

# Famous Skateboarders

Tony Hawk, from Carlsbad, California, made skateboarding famous. By age sixteen, he was the best skateboarder in the world. He retired in 1999 after performing the world's first two-and-one-half midair spin at the X Games. Tony now promotes skateboarding by building skateparks in new areas.

## Female skateboarders

Skateboarding is not just for boys. Elissa Steamer from Fort Myers, Florida, became a professional skateboarder in 1998. Elissa says, "When I started out, I never saw other girls at the skatepark. Now girls see skateboarding on television, and they want to be part of the action. If they want to follow me, I'm happy. I love my sport."

## Skate and snow

Snowboarding and skateboarding are similar sports. Shaun White of San Diego, California, proves that point. In 2003, Shaun won gold snowboarding in the Winter X Games and finished sixth in the skateboarding competition during the Summer X Games.

Elissa Steamer (right) and Evelien Bouilliart (left) won gold and silver, respectively, in the 2005 X Games.

## Skateboard facts - Did you know?

Skateboarders like to use slang: Brain bucket = helmet.
Bail = chicken out of a stunt. Fakie = riding backward.
Biff = crash. Carving = making turns on the skateboard.

Professional skateboarder Sergei Ventura of Norfolk, Virginia, is known for the amazing "air" he gets on his skateboard.

# TRUE STORIES

In 1998, Billy Copeland from Clarksville, Tennesee, reached a speed of 70 miles (112 kilometers) per hour on his board. Eight gas jets helped power his skateboard.

A new skatepark is planned.

Mounds of dirt form the ramps.

A worker sprays concrete over the base.

Workers smooth the surface.

The finished skatepark is in Lansing, Michigan.

# Boarding the Slopes

Snowboards range in length from 3 to 6 feet (90 to 180 cm). Freeride boards used for tricks and stunts let riders twist and turn down mountain slopes. Freecarve boards are designed to race down the mountains at high speeds.

Goggles protect the eyes from the glare of the snow.

## Halfpipe stunts

Snowboarders use halfpipes — U-shaped structures that look like a pipe cut the long way — made of hard-packed snow. Snowboarders slide down one side of the halfpipe to pick up speed. When they hit the top of the opposite wall, they get "air" for stunts.

**McTwist:** The rider performs a backflip with a twist in midair.

**Straight air:** The rider does a half-twist in the air, then rides back down the halfpipe wall.

**Grabs:** The rider grabs his or her snowboard during a trick.

Names for tricks include Slob Air, Stale Fish, and Fresh Fish.

## Snowboard facts - Did you know?

**Snowboarding started in the United States in the 1960s.**

**It has been an Olympic sport since 1998 and is now the fastest growing sport in the world.**

Shaun White from San Diego, California, is as talented on a snowboard as he is on a skateboard.

## TRUE STORIES

Nagano, Japan 1998. Nicola Thost of Pforzheim, Germany, won the first Olympic snowboarding gold medal for her halfpipe stunts.

Slopestyle

There are three kinds of snowboards:

Freeride snowboards are suitable for any mountain slope.

Freestyle snowboards are short, lightweight, and flexible, and great for airborne twists and turns.

Freecarve, or racing, snowboards are designed for making smooth turns at high speeds on hard snow.

# Snow Danger

Snowboard parks are great places to practice tricks. More daring freeriders would rather test their skills on steeper mountain slopes. Freeriders want to speed down the slopes, fly over ridges, jump into the air from high ledges – and then land on untracked snow below. These wild stunts are thrilling but dangerous. Freeriders need quick reactions to deal with trees, boulders, and steep cliffs.

## Avalanches

Snowboarding in remote areas can cause an avalanche. An avalanche – an enormous mass of tons (tonnes) of snow roaring down a moutainside at great speed – often occurs without warning. Snowboarders in remote areas must learn to recognize when avalanche conditions exist.

Freestyle snowboarders push themselves to the limit to perfect their favorite tricks.

## Safety gear

Snowboard safety gear includes a helmet, wrist guards, knee and hip pads, goggles, gloves, – and a satellite phone.

## Snowboard facts - Did you know?

Extreme snowboarders sometimes ride a helicopter to remote mountaintops. The only way back is down – by snowboard.

Freeride snowboarders
enjoy the extreme challenges
of wild mountain slopes.

## TRUE STORIES

Natalie and Chris Nelson from Mammoth
Lakes, California, are expert snowboarders.
This sister and brother team spends two
hundred days a year practicing new stunts.

Snowboard gear helps
prevent injuries.

Knee protectors
and shin guards.

Helmet with
detachable ear
warmers.

A thin hip pad
protects the
tailbone.

Gloves
with
good
grips.

# Around the World

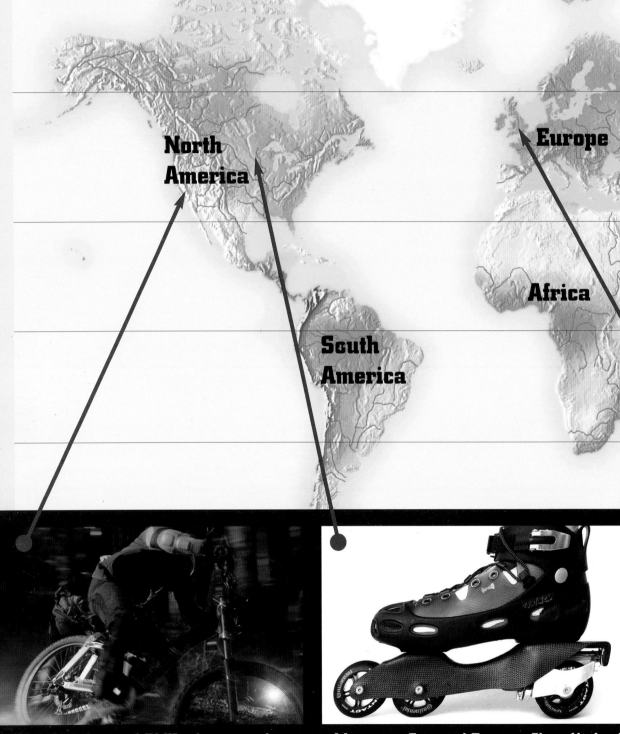

Skateboarding and BMX riding started in California.

Minnesota: Scott and Brennan Olson file for the first patent for modern in-line skates in 1979

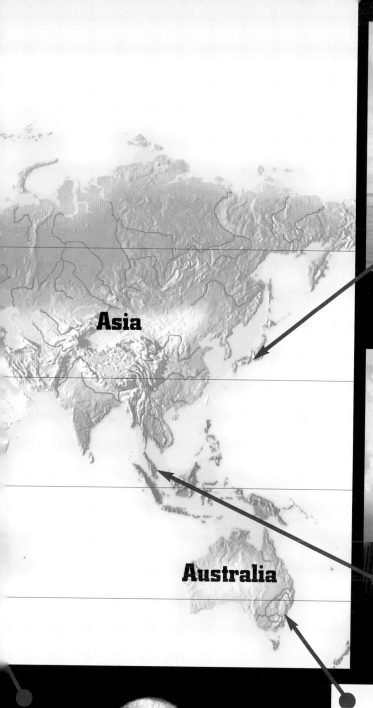

Asia

Australia

Nagano, Japan, 1998: Snowboarding became an official Olympic sport.

Kuala Lumpur, Malaysia, has hosted the Asian X Games since 2002.

London, England, 1760: Joseph Merlin is the first skater to use metal wheels.

Skateboarding star Jake Brown comes from Sydney, Australia.

# Glossary

**360 degrees:** a full circle.

**air:** to be off the ground while doing a trick.

**airborne:** flying through the air.

**athletes:** people who participate in sports.

**avalanche:** an overwhelming amount of snow that breaks loose and falls all at once down a mountainside, taking with it everything in its path.

**bearings:** metal balls inside the wheels of a skateboard to make them turn more easily.

**BMX:** bicycle motocross.

**bronze:** the color of the third-place medal.

**canyons:** in dirt biking, the dips between mounds on a dirt-bike jumping course.

**coping:** metal trim at the top of a ramp in a skatepark.

**deck:** the curved, wooden part of a skateboard.

**extreme:** pushed beyond common limits.

**flatland:** even, unbumpy terrain.

**frame:** the "skeleton" of a bicycle.

**fun box:** a ramp with four different slopes.

**gold:** the color of the first-place medal.

**goofy:** riding a skateboard or snowboard with the left foot foreward.

**griptape:** special skateboarding tape with a rough surface on one side that helps the skater's feet grip the board.

**halfpipe:** a ramp, made of wood or packed snow, shaped like a pipe cut in half lengthways.

**hardware:** the nuts and bolts used to join together the parts of a skateboard.

**handrail grind:** a skateboard stunt in which the rider slides the board along a rail or other object.

**in-line:** in a row.

**maple:** a type of wood used for most skateboards because of its flexibility and strength.

**mound:** a packed pile of dirt used for stunts.

**obstacle:** something blocking the way.

**ollie:** skateboard stunt invented by Alan "Ollie" Gelfand of Hollywood, Florida, in the early 1980s that takes the skateboard completely off the ground.

**parallel**: side by side but never touching.

**pogo stick**: a jumping toy with handlebars and footrests on either side of a springed stick.

**polyurethane**: a tough plastic used to make skateboard wheels.

**portable**: able to move around; not attached.

**professional**: someone who gets paid for work he or she does.

**remote**: far away from a developed area.

**Rollerblade®**: the commercial name for a brand of in-line skates; also, the term often used to refer to in-line skating on skates of any kind.

**satellite phone**: a portable phone that links to a satellite to make connections; best used in remote areas where cell phones are out of range.

**silver**: the color of the second-place medal.

**skatepark**: a concrete park with ramps that skaters use to practice and perform tricks and develop stunts.

**slang**: language or words used in place of more commonly accepted terms.

**snowboard**: a board somewhat like a skateboard, but without wheels, used for riding down snowy slopes.

**stalling**: pausing for a moment before continuing with a stunt.

**surfing**: using a board to ride large waves.

**tabletop**: a stunt that involves holding a bike parallel to the ground while in the air.

**terrain**: the type of landscape, such as rocky, smooth, hilly, or muddy.

**truck**: a metal device under a skateboard that holds the wheels and can be used for "grinding."

**vert**: short for vertical; used to describe stunts that use vertical ramps.

**wipeout**: to fall.

# Index